BRITAIN IN OLD PHOTOGRAPHS

AROUND
FAREHAM

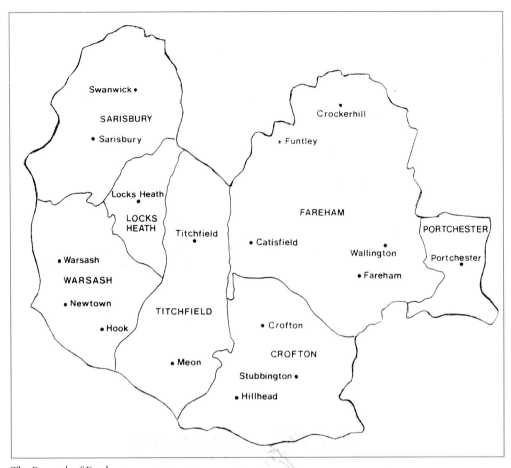

The Borough of Fareham.

All the proceeds from this book go towards the development of local history services in Westbury Manor Museum.

BRITAIN IN OLD PHOTOGRAPHS

AROUND
FAREHAM

OONAGH PALMER

SUTTON PUBLISHING LIMITED

Sutton Publishing Limited
Phoenix Mill · Thrupp · Stroud
Gloucestershire · GL5 2BU

First published 1998

Copyright © Oonagh Palmer, 1998

British Library Cataloguing in Publication Data
A catalogue record for this book is available from the
British Library.

ISBN 0-7509-1737-7

Typeset in 10/12 Perpetua.
Typesetting and origination by
Sutton Publishing Limited.
Printed in Great Britain by
Ebenezer Baylis, Worcester.

To Chris, Catherine and Jessica

A procession along West Street, Fareham, 1890s. The event which is being celebrated is uncertain, but this photograph is full of life and draws us back into a world before the car.

CONTENTS

ACKNOWLEDGEMENTS

Grateful thanks to the following sports clubs which helped provide photographs for the 'Sporting Times' chapter, which is based on a local history exhibition put on at Westbury Manor Museum in 1997: Fareham Wheelers Cycling Club, Portsmouth Hockey Club, Fareham Cricket Club, Portchester Cricket and Football Club.

I also wish to thank Anthony Triggs; Rural History Centre, Reading University; Aerofilms; Councillor F.A.J. Emery-Wallis; Mr Wyn Newbury and Mr Roy Knight from Warsash; the Portchester Society; Titchfield History Society; Mrs Brenda Clapperton and the Fareham Society; Mr Peagram for the use of some of his wonderful strawberry photographs; colleagues at Hampshire County Council Museums Service, particularly Bill Phillips, Wendy Bowen, Gill Arnott, Trevor Evans, Bob Holmes, Alastair Penfold; also John May, our freelance photographer, and special thanks are due to the Westbury Manor Museum assistants for their support, and to colleagues at Fareham Borough Council to whom the Museum is very dear.

Thanks are also due to Mrs Alice James and Fareham Local History Group, without whom much more of Fareham's history would be lost, and whose journal *Fareham Past and Present* is essential and enjoyable reading for people all over the Borough.

Bursledon Brickworks is now being restored by a charitable trust as a working museum and a Centre for the Built Environment. Thanks to Lynne Yates who lent me photographs and to her predecessor Diane Walker who produced such a good booklet on the Bursledon Brickworks.

Many thanks to Charlotte Matthews and Frank Green, from Hampshire Archaeology, who have added to our understanding of Cams Hall.

Thanks to the wonderful photographers of Fareham's past who have made books like this possible: J.T. See, Sidney Smith, F.G.O. Stuart, C.H. May, George Crouch and David Lawrence of Gosport, to name but a few.

And, above all, thanks to those many people throughout the Borough of Fareham who have donated objects, photographs and other materials to Westbury Manor Museum over the past few years, and to all those who will continue to do so in the future!

INTRODUCTION

This book aims to show some of the variety and wealth of history across the whole Borough of Fareham. The development of the Borough of Fareham as a political unit can be traced from the 1848 Public Health Act 150 years ago; it now includes Fareham, Titchfield, Crofton, Hillhead, Stubbington, Sarisbury Green, Hook with Warsash, Portchester, Locks Heath and Park Gate. Each of these areas has a rich history of its own, much of which has been researched by the network of local history groups which have worked hard to preserve the identities of their own particular areas in the face of the relentless changes which have occurred across the Borough in the last fifty years.

WESTBURY MANOR MUSEUM

The story of Westbury Manor as a building echoes the fortunes of the town of Fareham. Its core was a seventeenth-century farmhouse on the edge of Fareham. It was gentrified in the eighteenth century with an elegant Georgian façade and was further extended in the mid-nineteenth century. Research has shown that at least six admirals lived here and others are likely to have spent time in the house.

In 1932 Westbury Manor became the offices, or part of them, of Fareham Urban District Council and remained so, despite increasing pressure on space, until the new civic offices were built to accommodate the functions of the new Borough of Fareham. In 1976 Westbury Manor was left empty.

The demands of progress and the need to preserve the past came into conflict. The result for the building was increasing dereliction and fears for its future. However, fate played its part in the form of a bequest from Mrs Winifred Cocks, a local resident who left her house in Wickham Road, Fareham, to the Borough to be used as a museum. It was not very suitable for that purpose, but the proceeds from its sale were set up as a Trust and were used as a catalyst for a partnership between Fareham Borough Council and Hampshire County Council. The future of the building as the home for the Borough's museum was secured in 1986.

In 1990 Westbury Manor Museum opened in West Street, Fareham. Its aim was to tell the history of the whole Borough, not just that of the town of Fareham. The Curator, Alastair Penfold, relied extensively on the work of local history groups across the Borough as he worked to establish the museum. I have done the same with this book. As a relatively new museum our photographic archive is small but developing, and the collection of photographs in this book reflects the strengths and weaknesses of the museum collection as it stands.

In this collection of photographs, I have concentrated more on the way people spent their lives than on places. I am conscious that, as an 'incomer', there are people more qualified than I to comment on the changing environments. Nonetheless, I hope the photographs here will encourage people to delve deeper into the stories they represent. Westbury Manor Museum has a local studies area which has background material on most of the topics covered in the book and visitors are welcome either to browse or to make a more serious study of their interests.

I have checked the accuracy of the material included in this book as far as possible, and apologise if errors remain. I apologise also if I have inadvertently failed to make acknowledgement of the contribution of any individual or organisation.

CHAPTER ONE

OUT & ABOUT IN THE BOROUGH OF FAREHAM

The old Red Lion Inn, Stubbington, 1920s. In 1774 the Red Lion was advertising other services in the Hampshire Chronicle: 'This is to give Notice to all Gentlemen, Gamesters and others, that on Whit-Monday, at the Red Lion Inn, in Stubbington, will be played for, at Single Stick, One Guinea. The first best Man to have the Guinea, and the second best a Crown. And on Tuesday, the 24th instant, there will be a Bull baited, the dog that pins the Bull fairest to have Half-a Guinea.' It was a popular staging post in the 1890s for tourists visiting Warsash for the crab and lobster teas.

Portchester Castle, 1970s. Portchester became a popular place for people from Portsmouth and Southsea to visit, particularly after the building of the station in 1848. In August 1905 Portchester played host to a group of French sailors who were visiting Portsmouth as part of the celebrations to mark the Entente Cordiale of that year. Some of these sailors may have been descended from the French prisoners of war who spent many unhappy years imprisoned in Portchester Castle over the centuries.

The sailors arrive at Portchester station.

The Square, Castle Street, showing two of Portchester's public houses.

Walking up to the castle.

Tea in the castle grounds. It was obviously regarded as an important occasion with officers in full ceremonial dress. I wonder what the sailors made of it all!

Titchfield Abbey, *c.* 1950. Titchfield Abbey was founded in 1232 by Peter des Roches as a Premonstratensian monastery. After the Dissolution of the Monasteries in 1536 it was converted into Place House by its new owners, the Earls of Southampton. In 1741 the Titchfield Estates were bought by the Delme family who later purchased Cams Hall. Local traditions that they used stones and panelling from Titchfield Abbey for the Cams Hall alterations have little evidence in fact.

Titchfield Abbey, *c.* 1940: an aerial view showing the land around the Abbey under cultivation. The ruins that remain are those of the original Abbey to which further buildings were added to convert it into Place House. It is currently (1998) managed by the Titchfield Abbey Association on behalf of English Heritage and can be visited free of charge. It is also used as the venue for spectacular local events.

Old Houses in South Street, Titchfield, *c.* 1910. Some of the oldest houses in Titchfield are to be found in South Street, including a fourteenth-century storehouse converted in the sixteenth century into private dwellings.

High Street, Titchfield, *c.* 1910. The Queen's Head public house is still going strong.

The Square, Titchfield, *c.* 1905. There has to be a reason why these children, possibly from the National School, are photographed here in the Square. They look as if they are dressed in their best and are definitely posing for the camera.

Stubbington, *c.* 1910. This tranquil scene shows Binsted's grocers with the large Mazzawattee Tea sign and the Sun Inn.

The Crab and Lobster, 1916. In the 1880s Mr James Lock, a rag and bone man from Warsash who built up a fleet of crabbing boats, bought an old hulk and towed it to the shore at Warsash. He made alterations to the interior, named it the *Gypsy Queen*, and made it available for crab and lobster teas in the summer and dancing in the winter. As many as two hundred people a day would come to Warsash in charabanc loads at the height of the season.

The business prospered and more permanent premises were built next to the Rising Sun. The trade directories from the 1860s onwards only ever mention a Rising Sun public house in Warsash but it looks as though at one period at least it was known as the Sun Hotel. It too provided crab teas to meet the demands of local tourists. Local people who lived in the cottages off the shore also offered crab teas.

Fareham Creek, *c.* 1910.

Fareham Quay, 1930s. It looks so tranquil that it is hard to imagine that this is now the extremely busy Gosport Road. Fred Dyke's workshops under the viaduct can be seen in the distance.

Cams Mill, Fareham, *c.* 1910. This mill stood on the site of a much older one mentioned in the Domesday Book. Its picturesque appearance made it a popular topic for artists including Martin Snape, a famous Gosport artist. A painting of the mill by Valentine Garland is on display in Westbury Manor.

Cams Mill, *c.* 1919. The mill is obviously derelict and soon to be pulled down. The children here are Ivy and Cyril Wells with their aunt, Maud Smart.

CHAPTER TWO

HIGH DAYS & HOLIDAYS

Hook School, Warsash, c. 1900. Any visit from a photographer was a treat and an excuse to leave the classroom. Hook School was built in the 1870s by Arthur Hornby.

Processions to celebrate the great occasions of national life were a feature of Fareham life. This procession to celebrate the Coronation of George VI in 1937 is passing Westbury Manor, then the offices of Fareham Urban District Council, and features the magnificent floats of Tom Parker's Dairies. The Coronation festivities had been scheduled for the previous week but were rained off.

Children's fancy dress in the Coronation procession, 1937. As well as parades, the deferred Coronation festivities included a programme of sports at the Park Lane Recreation Ground. The day finished with a grand display of fireworks.

The Carnival Queen and her attendants, 1937. The Carnival Queen was Miss Vera Roffey.

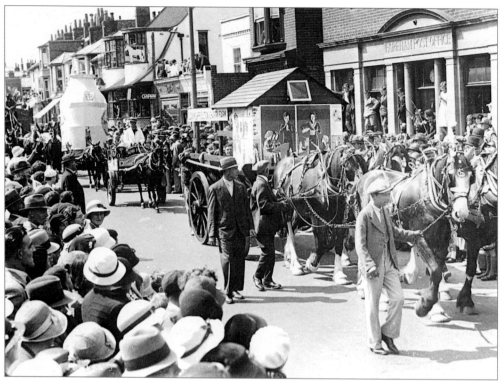

Magnificently decorated horses and carts from Tom Parker's Dairies formed an important part of any procession held in Fareham for most of the twentieth century. Tom Parker himself started farming at Charity Farm, north of Fareham, in 1921. He set himself up as a dairyman in 1928 so that he could sell his own produce direct to the public, and became hugely successful. He died in 1982.

The first May Queen pageant of the Portchester Woodcraft Chivalry in the grounds of Portchester Castle, 1950. This continued a tradition of historic pageants begun in 1907. Here the May Queen, Miss Ruby Saunders, arrives at the drawbridge.

Beefeaters escort the May Queen past her maids of honour.

Woodcraft boys and girls dance round the maypole.

Carnival day in Titchfield, *c.* 1890. The Titchfield Carnival became closely involved with the Bonfire Boys and is still going strong today.

George V Coronation celebrations at Titchfield, 1910.

Coronation celebrations in Titchfield, 1937. The banner at the end of the Square reads 'Long May He Reign'.

Coronation celebrations in Titchfield, 1937. Crowds are gathering outside Collihole's, a draper's shop in the Square, next to the Bugle Hotel.

A coach party leaving for Goodwood, outside the Coach and Horses, Titchfield, *c.* 1921, before the pub was rebuilt in 1925. This old inn at the bottom of Coach Hill has been traced back to 1780.

Sunday School treat waiting to go in Titchfield High Street, *c.* 1914. The Sidney House Drug Stores was owned by Arthur Ernest Mason who remained in business until at least the Second World War.

Titchfield peace celebrations, 1919. At this time no-one would think of going out for the day without a hat.

A baby show at Titchfield Fête, 1921.

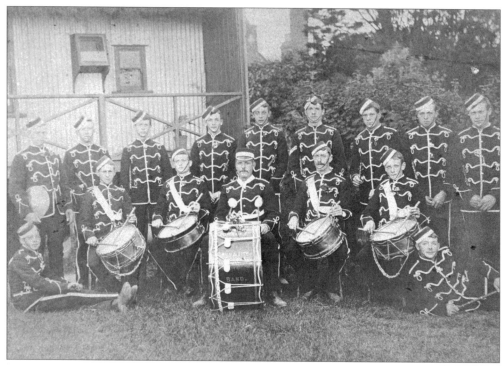

Fontley Fife and Drum Band, 1890s. Bands like this were very popular throughout the country and much in demand for processions on special occasions. The military-style uniforms added to the effect.

Relaxing in the beautiful gardens of The Potteries in Fareham, owned by Major Sandy who inherited the family pottery in 1906. His house, The Potteries, and its magnificent gardens were laid out in former clay pits. He frequently allowed it to be used for garden parties and fêtes. The pottery chimneys can be seen in the background.

CHAPTER THREE

STRAWBERRY FARE

*It is not known exactly where and when strawberries first became extensively cultivated in this area.
Certainly from the mid-nineteenth century they were an important facet of life in the Borough of Fareham,
particularly in the areas around Titchfield, Locks Heath, Park Gate, Swanwick, and Warsash. Here we have
a more unusual view of strawberry picking in Wicor Mill Lane, Portchester, c. 1931. In the background can
be seen the long chimney belonging to Wicor Bone Works.*

Strawberry growing in Swanwick, *c.* 1900. This photograph combines many of the elements of the strawberry industry in the area. Swanwick station is in the background with the grower, Mr Guest, his family and some of the pickers in the foreground. The horse and cart waits patiently outside the hut, which looks very new. A grower needed about 4 acres of land in order to make a living.

Strawberry pickers, *c.* 1900. At picking time every available person was co-opted to help, including schoolchildren who were given, or took, 'picking holidays'. It was essential that the grower picked and sold as many of the strawberries as possible, because he relied on the income to pay his debts and keep his family for the next year.

Gypsies were an important part of the labour force during the picking season. After the Wickham Fair, towards the end of May, many gypsies made their way to the strawberry fields of Titchfield, Locks Heath, and Warsash. This formally posed photograph of about 1905 of the grower's family and a gypsy family indicates a special occasion, possibly the baby's christening.

Most growers had a hut on their plot and here we see activity inside it. The men are putting covers on the baskets filled with strawberries ready to be distributed all over the country. The wicker baskets, known as 'gallons' and made by the inmates of Winchester gaol, held approximately 6 to 9 lb of fruit.

A familiar sight in the picking season as the strawberry carts queued to get into Swanwick station and load their produce on to a 'Strawberry Special'. The opening of Swanwick station in 1888 revolutionised the strawberry industry in the area by providing rapid transport to wider markets.

At least the station can be seen at the end of the line here! Many of the carts here may have been made by Hayter's of Portchester; a fine, and rare, example can be seen on display at Westbury Manor Museum.

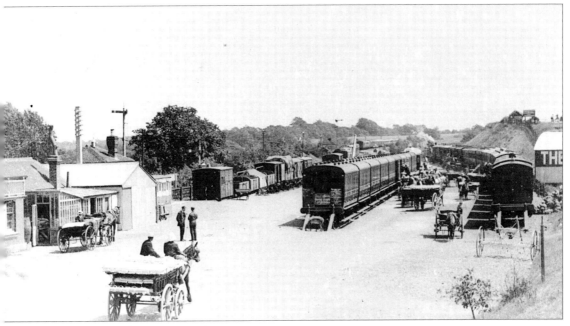

The yard at Swanwick station, *c.* 1910.

Swanwick station, *c.* 1918. The trains at Swanwick were loaded by teams of small boys who had to lie on their fronts to pack the specially constructed shelves in the railway carriages with baskets of strawberries. The cart in the foreground belongs to C.J. Newbury, a well-known Warsash firm which later used specially converted vans to transport strawberries to the London markets.

Picking in Locksheath, 1930s. The man holding the barrow is Reg Tucker who was well known for his involvement with local flower shows. If you look carefully you can see string tied round the waists of the pickers. This was used to attach empty baskets to their backs as they were working. The filled baskets were placed on the barrows to be collected at intervals by the grower. The extremely decorative hats worn by some of the women add a special charm to this photograph!

Strawberry season at Hollam Nurseries, Titchfield, 1928. Hollam Nurseries was owned by Mr E. Sanders.

Swanwick Basket Factory, *c.* 1915. In 1905 the Swanwick and District Growers' Association was formed by a group of local growers to help promote and sell their produce. In 1913 they set up the Swanwick Basket Factory in the goods yard behind Swanwick station to make the punnets, or 'chips', for the strawberries. These were non-returnable, and replaced the gallons.

The female workforce, *c.* 1915. The women were responsible mainly for assembling the chips.

Inside the Swanwick Basket Factory, 1940s. Here the men are pressing out the thin pieces of wood veneer from poplar logs, imported from the continent, which will be used to make the chips. The inner round logs which could not be turned into flat material were sold to shareholders for firewood. Later, cardboard and then plastic would be used to make punnets.

Making chips, 1940s. The women here are assembling the chips using a stapling machine. At this time, about sixty women were employed making baskets, but by 1964 there were only six.

CHAPTER FOUR

MEN AT WORK

Bursledon Brickworks, c. 1912. Bursledon Brickworks was founded in 1897 by Mr Ashby. There had been small local yards in the area but these had produced handmade bricks of 'not very good quality and supplies not very plentiful'. Bursledon used machinery, and experienced staff were brought in from Chandler's Ford Brickworks to run the new yard. The clay pits are in the foreground.

A kiln chamber and Mr Ashby, *c.* 1912. The chimney which served this kiln is still standing although the top 30 ft or so were removed some years ago for safety reasons.

Loading the kiln, *c.* 1912. After manufacture, the bricks were taken to large drying sheds where they remained for between ten days and three weeks. They were then barrowed to the kilns where they were loaded by hand for firing.

Loading the skips with clay to take it up to the machine sheds for processing. These skips travelled by their own weight to an inclined plane, where they were mechanically hauled into the engine house and tipped into a hopper above the pug mill.

The machine gang, 1922.

Employees at Bursledon Brickworks, *c*. 1925. All these men had served for twenty-five years. The brickworks remained a family-run business until it was amalgamated with the Sussex and Dorking Brick Company, eventually becoming Redlands Limited in 1959. It closed as a brickworks in 1974.

A group of clay diggers at Bursledon Brickworks, 1920s.

A group of workers at Bursledon Brickworks, late 1920s. Left to right: Tom Kite, Charlie Richards, Sammy Stares, George Hoare, George Read. George Hoare was the founder of G.W. Hoare & Sons, Builders.

Bursledon Brickworks outing.

Bursledon Brickworks First Football Team, *c.* 1932–4. Back row, left to right: Billy Whitter (Foreman), -?-, Bert Penney (kiln worker), Den Bevis, -?-, Charlie Welstead (digger), Reg Richards, Frank Lush (kiln worker), Bill Biddlecomb (kiln worker), George Rogers (kiln worker), 'Young' Roy Whitter, Ted Pratt. Front row: Mr Claude Ashby (owner), Sid Lush (kiln worker), Reg 'Dodger' Moore (kiln worker), Jimmy Spencer (kiln worker), Frank Penney (kiln worker), Fred Whitter (kiln worker), -?-.

Lower Swanwick Brickworks Cricket Club, winners of the Sarisbury and District Cricket League, Division II, Championship Shield, 1908. Back row, left to right: G. Turner, G. Pratt, T. Lockyer. Third row: G.W. Whitter, T. Pratt snr, N. Bevis, J. Sharp, J. Whitter, W. Whitter, A. Batley. Second row: ? Pratt jnr (standing), F. Bevis, A. Veck (Captain), S.R.S. Batley, W. Hayes, W. Mitchell, C. Hayes. Front row: A. Mitchell, F. Stubbs, A.R. Wise, A. White.

Loading the kiln at Fontley Brick Works, 1940s. The Brick and Tile Works operated for over a century at Fontley before closing in 1967. High-quality Fareham 'Red' bricks were produced here and transported all over the country and overseas. Prestigious buildings such as the Palmerston Forts and the Royal Albert Hall in London were constructed from these bricks. The works provided employment for a substantial number of local residents.

Grading tiles, early 1920s. The tiles are being offloaded from the barrows on to benches for sorting and stacking. Machine-made tiles were made at Fontley before the First World War. The clay used for the making of tiles was from a dark red seam. This seam was rock hard until exposed to water, when it became sticky and slippery but malleable. This could be very treacherous for the workers and at least three men were killed by falls of clay.

Tiles being loaded on to a railway wagon from a tile bogie at Fontley railway siding, early 1920s. They would be carefully packed in straw and transported round the country. Many tiles were also transported from Fareham Quay. Nearly all the work to do with the handling of the tiles was piece work. Left to right: Jack Watts, Tom Fleet, Ern Morris, Percy Adams.

Two workers at Fontley Brick and Tile Works enjoy a tea break, 1920s. This photograph shows a rare close-up of the huge kilns used in the production of bricks.

A group of workers from Fontley Brick and Tile Works, 1930s. The works provided one of the few places to find work during the recession.

Pottery was another very important clay-based industry in Fareham, particularly the manufacture of the famous Fareham chimney pots. The biggest pottery was the North Hill Potteries, started by the Sandy family in the nineteenth century. This rare photograph of about 1900 shows the clay being dug by hand from the clay pits before being transported to the mill, where it would eventually be crushed and pressed ready for the potter's wheel.

North Hill Potteries had two low sheds with a potter in each. Here the balls of prepared clay are waiting to be made into flower pots.

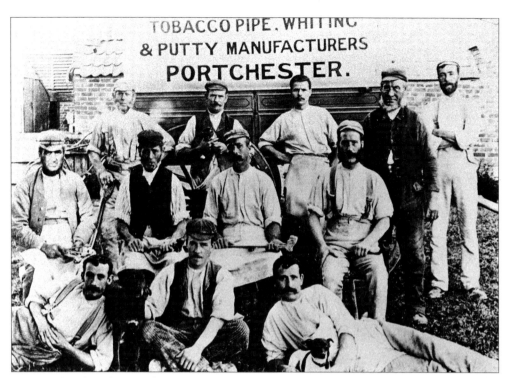

A group of workers from Leigh & Co. in Portchester, *c.* 1880. In 1840 Henry Leigh set up a factory in East Street for making clay pipes. The business later moved to Castle Street and became Leigh & Co. The man sitting in the centre is holding a mould for a very long-stemmed pipe much favoured by French fishermen.

Mr Henry Baker, the last clay pipe maker at Leigh's, prepares the mould for the pipe press. Carefully prepared clay was rolled into the rough shape of the pipe to be moulded. These were placed in groups of twelve on the dozening board, which can be seen on the right of the bench in this photograph.

The pipe press was loaded and closed. A press from Leigh's is on display at Westbury Manor Museum.

The excess clay forced out between the moulds was trimmed off. The pipes were then left to dry on a rack before being placed in saggars for firing at a temperature of about 900° Centigrade.

SPORTING TIMES

*Pyle's football team, 1921. The Pyle family were important members of Fareham's business community.
Many workplace teams joined Saturday and Wednesday Leagues. The young man second left on the back row
is William Bundey, aged seventeen.*

Portchester Football Team, 1894. This is believed to be one of the earliest team photographs. Portchester Cricket Club was founded in about 1886 or 1887, although it seems to have hit a bad patch in the 1890s. Portchester Football Club was officially established in 1894, although football had been played for many years before that. Portchester Cricket and Football Club remained as one organisation, sharing many of the same players and officials, until the 1960s.

Portchester Football Team, 1898. Back row, left to right: Hickey, Headley, Hayter, Moores, Sturgess, Marshall, Cathore. Middle row: Francis, E. Long, May. Front row: Marshall, Edgar ?, Gates, F. Long. Players at this time had to buy and maintain their own kit, which perhaps explains the interesting variety of socks!

Portchester Football Team, 1908/9. Portchester Football Club entered the Portsmouth Football League in 1903 in Division Three. In 1909 they were in Division Two, winning the league title that year and being promoted to Division One. Back row, left to right: Marshall, Budd, Perry, Hayter, Durant, Carter, Marchant, Sturgess. Middle row: Adams, Ponting, Hayter, Gates, Jeffery, Martell. Front row: Puckett, Francis.

Portchester Football Club, 1935/6. Portchester were back in Division One at this time, attracting nearly 100 spectators at home matches. One of the particular constraints of playing against the magnificent backdrop of Portchester Castle was the need to clear the ground before the games could start, because cows were allowed to graze in the outer bailey of the castle during the week. Back row, left to right: A. Durant, D. Page, Lewer, Godwin, Rand, -?-, Bartlett, Rand, R. Adams. Middle row: B. Page, James, Admiral Smith, Godwin. Front row: Russell, Hannat, Pratt.

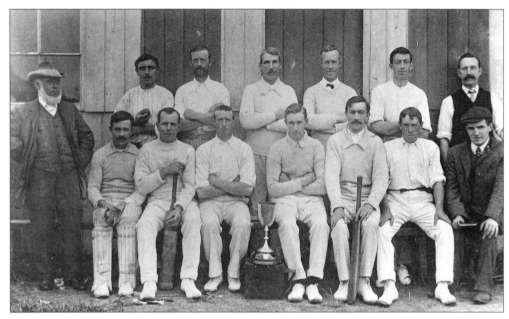

Portchester Cricket Club, 1908. Back row, left to right: Puckett, Bone, Pelling, Sibley, Martell, Perry. Front row: Hunt, Sturgess, Carter, Durant, Pratt, Russell, Marchant. The man with the beard on the left is Mr Marshall.

Portchester Cricket Club, 1919. Back row, left to right: H. Hannat (Committee); C. Meatyard, T.L. Marchant (Hon. Sec.), F.J. Hawkins, C.E. Long (Committee), L. Gates, E.G. Martell, -?-, Hayward (Committee). Middle row: A.E. Durant (Hon Treasurer), B.C. Gates (Vice-Capt.), J.J. Rogers (President), Revd H.E.K. Fry (Captain), S.P. Moorey. Front row: J. Russell, G. Pratt.

Portchester Cricket Club, 1955. Back row, left to right: T. Sparshott, H. Price, R. Adams, T. Robinson, R. Harris, D. Williams. Middle row: G. Savage, F. Ridge, G. Russell, G. Wilkinson Snr, W. Wiseman. Front row: G. Wilkinson, G. Durant, B. Spall, K. Loader, Mrs Russell (scorer).

Fareham and District Hockey Team, 1900/1. The club was formed in 1899 and is one of the oldest hockey clubs in Hampshire. Back row, left to right: S.W. Perrott, P.G. Pollard, G.A. Thomas, R.W. Napier, S.E.P. Weatherhead. Front row: P. Case, N.M. Atkins, J.R. Wyatt, M.D. Brook (Captain), G. Simpson, C.E. Atchison.

Fareham Ladies Hockey Club at Stubbington Recreation Ground, late 1960s. There was a Fareham Ladies Hockey Club in existence in the 1920s but all trace seems to have disappeared. However, a new club was formed in September 1954 by Trixie Morgan, a teacher at Wykeham House School, Fareham.

Fareham Ladies Hockey Club, thirtieth anniversary, 1984. On the back row are Trixie Morgan, Fareham Mayoress Mrs Margaret Jerrard, and President Di Hill.

Warsash football team, 1920s. They were obviously successful, judging by the cup!

Fareham Bowling Club, 1930s. In the first half of the twentieth century Fareham had a thriving bowling club which used to meet at the White Horse Hotel in West Street. It seems to have disbanded in the late 1950s or 1960s. The current, very successful, Fareham Bowling Club was formed in 1974 as a mixed club.

The recreation ground at Bath Lane was opened in May 1887 and extended in 1903, when Fareham Urban District Council bought allotments at the far end of the ground. An article in the *Hampshire Post* of 1913 commented that 'a gentleman who has visited almost all parts of the world was impressed by the beauty of the scene to be obtained from the pavilion when the tide is in and cricketers and tennis players are engaged in their respective pastimes on the "Rec".'

A school outing at the recreation ground, Titchfield, *c*. 1925. The recreation ground was established in 1897 to mark Queen Victoria's Diamond Jubilee. Initially vandalism proved to be a great problem, occupying much of the time of the Parish Council in the early years of the twentieth century.

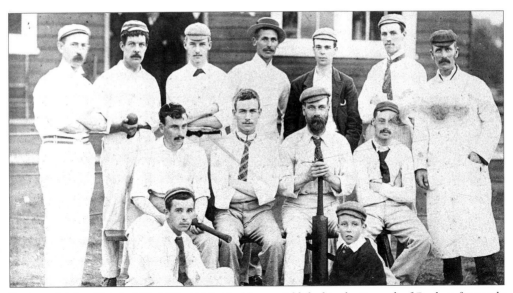

Fareham Cricket Club 2nd XI, 1891. Cricket had been established in the Borough of Fareham for nearly 200 years before the establishment of Fareham Cricket Club in 1882; its home ground was behind Trinity Church. The club was very successful in the 1890s. Back row, left to right: C. Clark, A. Wareham, Percy Weatherhead, H. Chappell, A. Osgood, H. Coghlan, A. Stead (Umpire). Middle row: B. Champness, E. Edmunds, H. Smith, Bert Gale. Front row: W. Osgood, Horace Smith (scorer).

Winners of the Gosport Shield, 1910 and 1911. Fareham Cricket Club disbanded in 1904 but another team of cricketers called the 'Fareham Early Closers' took the name of Fareham Cricket Club, with Bath Lane Recreation Ground as their home ground. This new Fareham Cricket Club joined the Gosport and District League in 1910, winning the First Division Shield in 1910 and 1911. Back row, left to right: W. Pharo (Groundsman), Godwin (Scorer), E. Frost, Mr Calder, W. Cummins, R. Child. Middle row: Mr A. Brewer (Umpire), W. Kiddle, P. Stedham, H. Smith, E. Edmunds (Capt), Harry Abraham, Percy Pink. Front row: Denis and Donald Edmunds, ? Evans, Fred Woodward, R. Smith, Donald Pink, Jack Pharo.

Fareham Wheelers, 1946/7. Left to right: John Hayles, John Gauntlet, Peter Press, Nellie Ludford, Fred Moore, Larry Austin. The Fareham Wheelers Cycling Club was founded in 1927 by Mr E.J. Cambrai, a master baker from Titchfield, after young cyclists persuaded him that a cycling club was needed in the town. Early activities revolved around Sunday club rides, touring and general socialising. The club reformed after wartime disruption in 1946 and is still going strong today.

John Hill and George Salisbury of the Fareham Wheelers, late 1930s. Both worked at the accounts office for Fareham Urban District Council from 1936 to 1940.

Fareham Wheeler Belles, 1950s. The Fareham Wheelers had a tradition in their early days of encouraging women cyclists.

Nellie Ludford near Grove Road, West Street, Fareham, taking part in a 10 mile Time Trial, 1947.

The Gosport and Fareham Beagles Hunt was established in about 1866 by a group of local gentry. The kennels were built near the Windmill Inn at Peel Common. Regular meets were held across the Borough.

The hunt was not always successful as this extract from a report in the *Hampshire Post* of 1913 describes: 'On arriving at the marshes, the dogs were quickly on the scent, but after a short run, they lost the hare and turned out another in an adjoining field, which promised to give a fine run had it not been caught in the barb wire on clearing the hedge.'

Meet of the otter hounds in the Square, Titchfield, early 1900s.

The Boxing Day Hunt traditionally met outside Fareham's Railway Hotel, which can be seen in the background here, *c.* 1936. Mr William Sandy, Master of the Hunt, is on the horse.

Netball team, Senior Girls School, Harrison Road, early 1930s. Back row, left to right: Hazel Stead, Cynthia Salisbury, Vera Bartlett, Aileen Salisbury. Front row: Betty Johns, Eileen Maynard, Mabel White, Joan Cruft, Betty Pink.

Senior Girls School, Harrison Road, early 1930s. Aileen Salisbury and Mabel White are dressed for tennis. The Senior Girls School in Harrison Road was opened in 1930 with Miss D.A. Ings as headmistress. A new boys senior school was opened in 1933 with Mr G.W. Simms as headmaster.

Physical exercises at Harrison Road School, early 1930s. The divided skirts are very different from the range of sports kit worn by girls today, but they were standard sports uniform right through until the 1980s.

The range of sport and physical education offered to girls has increased enormously over the past decade.

The crew of the *Dorris* at Fareham Quay, *c*. 1902. Fareham Sailing Club has a long and successful history. Its origins lie in the Fareham Rowing Club which was active in the 1850s, but it may be even older than that. Fareham Sailing Club shared the organisation of Fareham's annual regatta for many years.

Bathing in Fareham Creek had long been popular, although by the time this photograph was taken by Sidney Smith in the 1930s pollution had made it a much less desirable pastime. A sea water bathing house was built in 1838 at a cost of £600 but this had disappeared by the 1890s. In 1979 a swimming pool was built in Park Lane.

CHAPTER SIX

SERVING THE PEOPLE

Titchfield Waterworks, c. 1906. The gentleman here is reputed to be Mr King. The provision of water is a serious business for any community. Some people in Titchfield had their own wells but the water was often not fit to drink. Fareham Rural District Council paid people like Mr King to travel around with a donkey supplying drinking water at one farthing per 2 gallon bucket of water.

Here we see a collection of town characters, including a couple of telegraph boys and possibly a butcher posing for a photograph by the pump.

Titchfield 'Waterworks' at a slightly later date. The notice reads: 'Any person damaging this pump or wasting the water will be prosecuted. By Order, Rural District, Fareham.' Mains water was brought to Titchfield in 1922 and 1923. The cottage which is behind the pump in the photograph above was knocked down in 1908.

Titchfield Night Watchman, *c*. 1890. This is thought to be Mr Burgess, who also worked as the Town Crier until about 1915.

Post office at Stubbington, *c*. 1905. The post office was in the hands of the Binsted family from the 1870s. This photograph shows the mail either being delivered or collected.

Fareham Volunteer Fire Brigade, *c.* 1895. They are pictured here with their smart new steam engine, purchased in 1894 from Shand, Mason & Co. at a cost of £306. Shand & Mason were an old-established firm that had been making fire engines since 1774. The new 'steamer' went on trial in November 1894, creating much public interest; the tests ended with a parade through the town.

The opening of the new fire station in West Street, 1911. The Fareham Volunteer Fire Brigade was formed in 1889 with a station in Quay Street. Arthur Sutton joined in this year, and was promoted to the rank of Captain by 1894 when the Urban District Council took over town affairs from the Local Board of Health. He had campaigned for many years for this new fire station.

The fire station in West Street, *c.* 1912. This view shows, from left to right, the parish hall, the fire station, United Reformed church, and Portland Chambers.

Hants County Asylum Fire Brigade, pictured here with their Merryweather fire engine, 1880s. Merryweather's were also a long-established firm and were the main rivals to Shand & Mason. Merryweather's tender for the Fareham Fire Brigade had been £342, as opposed to Shand & Mason's £306!

Nurses at Knowle Hospital, 1930s. This hospital opened in December 1852 as Hampshire County Asylum, with 400 inmates. It was a self-contained community in many ways, with its own laundry, needle room, boot and shoe repair shop – and cemetery. In 1899 it was taken over by Hampshire County Council, and in 1921 its name was changed to Knowle Mental Hospital.

Nurse Mary Ann Cresswell, *c.* 1932. Nurse Cresswell was a well-known midwife in the Fareham District, which included Fareham, Fontley, Catisfield and Portchester. She was responsible for delivering over 3,000 children during her career and was well known for travelling on her tricycle, with her black medical bag strapped to the carrier, in all weathers to see her patients. She retired in 1937, aged seventy.

St Christopher's Hospital, Wickham Road. This was originally the site of the Fareham Union Workhouse, built in the 1830s under the requirements of the 1834 Poor Law. Fareham Workhouse operated a benevolent regime on the whole, although a scandal involving the treatment of three small boys was uncovered as research was being done before the establishment of Westbury Manor Museum. In 1948 it became St Christopher's.

The wheelwright's shop at Hook, *c*. 1908. The sign reads 'C.J. Newbury. Building Contractor, Wheelwright, Undertaker, Decorator. Estimates Given.' Much of the wood used came from the Hook Park Estate. Newbury's became an important builder in the area and, at one stage, employed about a hundred men.

Newbury's employees, *c*. 1910. From about 1875 Newbury's was responsible for most of the building work in Warsash, Hook, Locks Heath area.

The village blacksmith at Hook, *c.* 1906. The blacksmith's forge here was occupied by generations of the Sylvester family from at least 1814 until the death of Mr Arthur Sylvester in 1964. Wooden wheels made in the wheelwright's shop would be rolled to the forge to be completed with the fitting of iron tyres.

The *Stella* and *Cupid*, *c.* 1907. These were two of the crabbing boats owned by James Lock that operated from Warsash from the 1860s until the early years of the twentieth century. The boats were adapted for this purpose by having their holds sealed, with watertight bulkheads being fitted. Holes were drilled into the sides and bottom of the boat to keep the water circulating to provide storage for the live crabs and other shellfish, which were collected from Devon and Cornwall, France and Ireland.

St Edith's Home for Girls, *c.* 1929. St Edith's was built in 1907, replacing the Church of England Society of Homes for Waifs and Strays which had been in existence in one form or another since 1869. There were usually about twenty girls in residence, who were trained in domestic skills so that they could find work as servants. The building is now the Roundabout Hotel.

Pyle's Temperance Commercial Hotel was established in the 1880s by Edward Pyle. By 1915 it was in the hands of J. Herbert Pyle. In 1908 it was offering 'Good Accommodation for Large or Small Parties' and 'Spacious Dining and Refreshment Rooms'.

CHAPTER SEVEN

TRAVEL & TRANSPORT

Mr Koosens and his car, c. 1900. Mr Koosens of Southsea imported a Lutzmann car from Germany in November 1895. This car proved to be very troublesome, having engine problems. He went on a drive to Lee-on-Solent and came back through Fareham — where he was caught driving without a red flag ahead. He was fined 1s and costs of 15s 7d by the 'silly old magistrate'!

Percy See's waterside premises, 1930s. Percy See (1881–1944) spent most of his life at the cutting edge of boat design. He realised the potential of the internal combustion engine at an early date and was a major producer of record-breaking racing hydroplanes.

Two of Percy See's boats. As well as his work at the forefront of marine technology, Percy See also catered for the ordinary leisure sailing market.

An unexpected biplane landing in Locks Heath Park, *c.* 1913. This was a military biplane whose pilot landed to visit his fiancée who lived in the area. The plane took off the next day but apparently had difficulty in summoning up enough speed in the limited space of the park. The man wearing the panama hat and with the pony and trap is thought to be Mr Louis Lynn, a familiar and respected figure in the area.

A selection of Fred Dyke's vehicles beside the viaduct at Fareham. Dyke's had a workshop under the arches of the viaduct where the vehicles were kept in the 1920s and 1930s (see p. 17).

'Teddy', owned by Fred Dyke, photographed at the Fareham and Hants Show at Roche Court, August 1934.

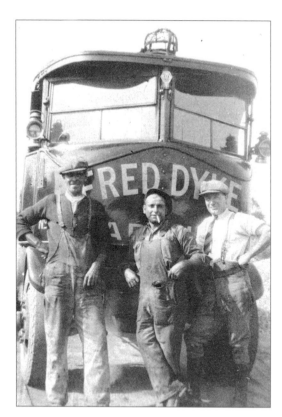

A group of Fred Dyke's workers with a Sentinel steam lorry, *c.* 1938. In the years after the First World War, Mr Dyke's growing business in Fareham included refuse collection, gravel and general haulage and furniture removals.

Fred Dyke's repair shop at Lower Quay, *c.* 1935. This view also shows Fareham Flour Mill and the large grain store, built in 1910 for Thomas Gater & Co. Ltd.

In this scene at Lower Quay the horse and cart waits to transport goods, possibly from Wood & Co.'s flat-bottomed barge seen here laden with coal.

Workers from Wood & Co. at Fareham Quay, their carts laden with sacks of coal, *c.* 1885. The viaduct is just visible in the background. The Coal Exchange pub on Lower Quay is named after the important coal trade. This photograph provides rare evidence for working men's costumes of the period.

The railway siding at Bursledon Brickworks, 1912. When the bricks were ready, they were transported along the River Hamble or by rail. A spur from the main railway line which passes the works was brought into the yard at Bursledon, so that bricks could be easily loaded and distributed throughout the country.

The *Langstone, c.* 1912–20. Barges like this were used to transport bricks down the Hamble. An aerial ropeway took the bricks down to the Bursledon Brick Company's quay on the Hamble. Note the loaded brick barrow on the quay.

Wallington Brewery, early 1900s. The Wallington Brewery was bought by the Saunders family in 1867 and remained in their ownership until 1944. Deliveries were made weekly to the public houses owned and served by the family as well as to some of the more important landed gentry. Deliveries were made by horse-drawn drays until about 1929. One particular favourite was a grey called 'Goosey'.

Delivering Saunders' beer to the Miner's Arms in Fontley. The landlord, Jim Feast, is in the doorway and the drayman is John Becket. Jim was landlord from 1890 to 1913.

Women tram crew, *c.* 1916. Gosport and Fareham Tramways hired a number of female drivers and conductors in the First World War. In smart navy uniforms, they braved the elements as they did their bit for the war effort. Miss Gladys Hayes is the driver and Miss Ward is the conductor.

Provincial tram terminus at Fareham station, early twentieth century. Trams were a cheap and popular form of travel with tradesmen of the time who needed plenty of space for their tool bags. The old tram lines, in the middle of the road, did not have any buffers so the end of the line had to be approached with some care. The tram terminus at Fareham station tended to be an accident blackspot.

Charlie Smith's bus, *c.* 1927. Charlie started the first Fontley–Fareham–Knowle bus service in 1926. The chimneys behind the bus belong to Fontley Brick and Tile Works' continuous brick kiln.

Swanwick station after the rush, *c.* 1905. The gallons are waiting collection by growers, and will be stored ready for next year's picking season. In 1913 Swanwick station could handle in excess of 100,000 baskets of fruit a day in specially adapted trains. The last 'Strawberry Special' ran in 1966.

Fareham station, *c*. 1910. The station opened in 1841 when the first extension of the London to Southampton Railway allowed trains to run from Eastleigh through Botley and Fareham to Gosport. The line had to be closed four days after it opened because the tunnel was thought to be unsafe. It was eventually reopened in February 1842.

Fareham station, *c*. 1910. Cattle trucks can be seen in the sidings on the left. The extension of the railway line to Portsmouth in 1848 required the building of Fareham's seventeen-arch viaduct to carry trains across the Creek.

Portchester station was opened in 1848 when the line was extended from Fareham to Portsmouth. The station is built of brick and flint in the style of a castle. Many long-distance travellers used this station when they visited Portchester Castle before increasing numbers of cars led to road improvements.

Knowle Halt, 1950s. Knowle Halt was built in 1907 to service Knowle Hospital. It was very busy on visiting day, and all the coal for the hospital boilers was also brought by rail to this Halt.

Bursledon Bridge, *c.* 1900. In 1797 the Bursledon Bridge Company received permission by Act of Parliament to build a toll bridge across the Hamble. The original Bursledon Bridge was an attractive wooden one.

At each end of the bridge there was a painted sign setting out the various tolls. In 1930 Hampshire County Council bought the bridge from the Bursledon Bridge Company and freed it from tolls. In 1933–5 it was replaced by a concrete structure.

Warsash with ferry, *c.* 1948. There had long been a ferry crossing between Warsash and Hamble.

Park Gate Garage, *c.* 1930.

CHAPTER EIGHT

SHOPPING

An engraving by C.S. Shepherd of West Street, Fareham, 1830s. When the buildings in the centre were demolished in the 1850s West Street was such a wide and imposing thoroughfare that it became the main trading street for the town and the surrounding area for many years. It was so busy and affluent that it became known as the 'Golden Mile'.

Herbert Rodgers and Mr Miles on the milk float, *c.* 1910. Herbert Rodgers worked for Mr Miles' Dairy, situated next to the school on the corner of Abshot Road. He did the daily deliveries in the Titchfield Common/Locks Heath area with a horse called 'Joe'.

Delivering meat to Hook, *c.* 1908. The cottages at Hook were built in about 1846 for workers on the Hook estate. The wheelwright's shop with the cart in front was run by Newbury's.

J. Herbert Pyle came to Fareham in the 1880s as a partner in a bakery and confectionery business owned by his uncle William Pyle. William Pyle is first mentioned in the trade directories in the 1870s. J.H. Pyle bought the old Paragon Hotel at 31 West Street, Fareham, and converted it to the Paragon Bakery sometime around 1895.

Pyle's delivery service, c. 1915. Delivering goods, especially to their well-to-do customers, was an essential part of any business.

Pyle's delivery service, *c.* 1927. The horse and cart has given way to the van but the big bread baskets remain the same. By the 1920s the business was known as Pyle & Son.

Busy West Street, Fareham, *c.* 1905.

Even busier West Street, 1950s. Tom Parker's milk float is parked outside Lusby & Son, both now part of Fareham history. Silver's closed in 1996.

Lankester & Crook, Titchfield, *c.* 1937. These were the largest grocers, at the corner of the Square and West Street. They sold everything from bacon to paraffin and groceries of all kinds. The wonderful smells of shops like that are a thing of the past, a far cry from the antiseptic supermarkets of today.

High Street, Fareham, early 1930s.

High Street, late 1930s. This is taken from a postcard postmarked 1941. The message, written in a child's hand, reads: 'Please send coupons be ok write later love Bill.' Abraham's has gone, to be replaced by Pilcher's.

The Little Dustpan, *c.* 1905. This was a shop
owned for many years by Mr Edmund
Abrahams, one of Fareham's best-known and
respected tradesmen. He died in 1923 but his
son carried on the business until 1938. The
Little Dustpan was located next door to
Westbury Manor, and a furnishings store
continued on the site until 1993, when it was
demolished as part of the town centre
redevelopment.

Abraham's emporium, 1930s. This was located in the High Street, and owned by W.G. Abraham, from
another branch of the 'Little Dustpan' Abraham family. It was a successful upholstery and cabinet maker's
business but they also acted as undertakers and agents for Gilbey's wines and spirits.

Lusby's, c. 1930. Lusby's was a high-class grocer with two shops in West Street, at nos 7 and 167. Valued customers would draw up outside in coaches and carriages and staff would go out and take their orders. Lusby's also had a packing store in East Street where the larger and country orders were packed ready for delivery by horse-drawn delivery vans, later by motor vans. Lusby's main shop was sold in 1955.

Service with a smile – Lusby's staff, 1950s. This photograph evokes the days of shopping before the supermarket.

An aerial view of West Street, Fareham, *c.* 1941. The market-place with the animal sheds is clearly visible; it is now a car park. Westbury Manor can be seen shrouded by trees, with the council yards following the line of Hartlands Road. Westbury Manor's Victorian-style garden and the bus station now occupy this area.

Fareham market, *c*. 1910. In 1795 a public meeting established that a market should be held every Monday fortnight, but there had been markets here since the Middle Ages.

Fareham market, *c*. 1910. Animals would be driven in 'on the hoof' the day before and kept in the fields and pounds in the north of the town. They were then driven through the town, causing chaos. A market company purchased land which became the livestock market for many years, replacing its previous site outside the old Town Hall in West Street.

CHAPTER NINE

IN THE NICK OF TIME

Roche Court, 1930s. Roche Court has a long and varied history, having passed through the hands of the Bishops of Winchester, the des Roches family and eventually the Admiralty. In 1961 it became the home of Boundary Oak School, a local preparatory school. Finding new uses for historic buildings is often the only way to secure their futures.

Westbury Manor in West Street, as it was in 1990 when it opened as a museum. The original core of the building is seventeenth century. The façade is Georgian, while the wings and rear bay are Victorian extensions. Westbury Manor is reputed to have been the home of at least six admirals before it became the offices of Fareham Urban District Council in 1932. The frontage has since been graced with an elegant eighteenth-century carriageway and railings.

The derelict front of Westbury Manor, 1987. The notice in the forecourt says: 'As from 1st September this area will no longer be available for parking due to building works. Please use the next motor cycle parking area 50 yards east.' Definitely a sign that things were about to change!

The derelict rear of Westbury Manor, 1987. Once Fareham Borough Council moved to the Civic Offices in 1975–6, the future of Westbury Manor became uncertain. It was the bequest from a local resident, Mrs Winifred Cocks, which provided the catalyst for a partnership arrangement between Hampshire County Council and Fareham Borough Council to convert the building into a museum for the Borough of Fareham.

The rear of Westbury Manor after restoration, 1990. A beautiful Victorian-style garden, managed by Fareham Borough Council, has now replaced the wire fencing.

Father Christmas visiting Westbury Manor, Christmas 1962.

The war may have been over, but Civil Defence was still a high priority. A small-scale Civil Defence Emergency Feeding Exercise took place at Westbury Manor on 4 March 1954. Cooking was done on an improvised brick-built combined hot plate and oven and with a simple trench cooker. 'An excellent lunch consisting of soup, fish pie followed by a baked pudding, was prepared.' From left to right: Mrs E.L. Fritchley, Mr W.T.J. Crick, Cllr K.J. Riley (Chairman of Fareham Urban District Council), Mr B.W. Rands, Mrs A. Boniface tending the fire, helped by Mrs A. Dale.

The Chairman of Fareham Urban District Council, Cllr K.J. Riley, has a word with members of Fareham WVS who are working at the improvised hot plate and oven cooker. From left to right: Mrs E.L. Fritchley, Mrs M.E. Albrow, Mrs E.F. Tatford, Mrs H. Bishop, Mrs F. Dyke and Mrs M. Horner, kneeling.

Westbury Manor played its part in the war effort. Mr W. Rands, from Fareham Urban District Council, is presiding over the second issue of ration books in June 1940.

Westbury Manor from across West Street, late 1930s.

A view of Westbury Manor garden when it was a private residence, 1920s.

Cams Hall, *c.* 1936. Cams Hall, near Fareham, was another building which nearly came to a sad end. A house has stood on this site for several hundred years but in the late eighteenth century it was substantially rebuilt in its present style by the architect Jacob Leroux for its owner John Carnac.

The rear of Cams Hall, *c.* 1936. In 1781 the house was bought by the colourful Delme family, who lived there for a hundred years before the estate passed into the hands of a succession of owners and tenants.

The kitchen at Cams Hall, *c.* 1936. The spartan nature of the kitchen provides a contrast to the opulence elsewhere. There are few 'mod cons' apparent here, although Cams Hall had electricity installed in the early twentieth century.

Another part of the kitchen was described thus by John David Spinney: 'dressers against south and west walls, loads of crockery and glowing copper moulds, and a fascinating coffee grinder'. Mr Spinney took a series of photographs of Cams Hall in 1936 soon after the death of his grandmother, Mrs Ramsay, who had lived in the house for many years. The collection belongs to Fareham Borough Council but copies of the photographs and their accompanying commentary can be consulted at Westbury Manor Museum.

The smoking room.

The conservatory.

This magnificent Adam-style marble fireplace, originally located in the smoking room, is now in Westbury Manor Museum after being rescued by Fareham Local History Group from a near derelict Cams Hall in the 1960s. The four heads represent the four seasons but the mythological scene above the mantelpiece is something of a mystery. The under-housemaid had to clean this fireplace with a toothbrush!

Cams Hall tracers, 1945. The tracers worked for the Admiralty at Cams Hall during the war, after they were evacuated from Portsmouth dockyard. Left to right: Margaret Bell, Miss Preston, Bushy, Pamela, Joyce, Pearl, Ella, Rosemary.

Time to relax, early 1940s.

Cams Hall, late 1950s. When the Admiralty left the building in 1949 it was in excellent condition but then began a process of decline. This photograph shows broken windows and a general air of desolation.

Artistic dereliction, 1991. As Cams Hall became increasingly neglected there were fears for its survival. Luckily it was saved through the intervention of Strand Harbour Securities who restored the outer building. Trevor Evans, Hampshire County Council Museums Service's photographer, and Bob Holmes, a Hampshire County Council Museums Service conservator, made a photographic survey of the building over about five years, recording both its derelict state and its restoration.

Alastair Penfold and Mrs Alice James survey the scene at Cams Hall, 1991. A detailed study of the archaeology of the standing building was conducted by Hampshire Archaeology Limited of Romsey. In this photograph we can see good examples of eighteenth-century bricks blocking up four seventeenth-century windows. These are some of the clues that show there has been a building on this site for several centuries.

The stables at Cams Hall, 1991. These stables are remarkable for the very ornate capitals on the columns which divide the stalls. Their origin is mysterious. There is a possibility that they were taken from Place House, formerly Titchfield Abbey, but no definite proof of this has come to light.

Cams Hall, 1990. At this stage the building had deteriorated to such an extent that it was only the scaffolding which prevented the complete collapse of the outer walls. A restored Cams Hall now occupies its traditional place in the local landscape.

CHAPTER TEN

VANISHED SPLENDOURS

The Hook, c. 1838. The Hook was built by Sir William Hornby, a former Governor of Bombay, when he returned to England in 1783 as a wealthy and prosperous man. He bought land in the Hook area and built himself a palatial mansion, reputed to be a copy of the Governor's Mansion he had occupied in Bombay. The Hook burnt to the ground in 1903.

Warsash House, *c.* 1916. The estate agent's particulars for the sale of the Warsash Estate describe Warsash House thus: 'The Mansion is built of Brick, with part rough cast and part stuccoed exterior, and with pan-tiled roof. It has an imposing appearance, and the site it occupies is unrivalled in the south of England, being on an elevation, with attractive Park and Meadows sloping to the River Hamble, over which and Southampton Water it has Magnificent Views.'

The hall at Warsash House, 1916. Warsash House was designed by Sir Frederick Leighton in the mid-nineteenth century and occupied for forty-five years by the family of Algernon Sartoris, and by Mr G.A. Shenley from the 1890s. The Warsash Estate was finally bought by a land company in 1934 and Warsash House was pulled down in 1937. The ceiling is panelled with oak beams, while the open hearth is surrounded by tiles and a beautifully carved stone mantelpiece showing a boar hunt in the forest.

The drawing room of Warsash House, 1916. It opened into the conservatory and overlooked the Italian garden.

The library, Warsash House, 1916.

The Japanese room, Warsash House, 1916. There were seven other major bedrooms, some with *en suite* bathrooms. The servants' bedrooms were mainly on the second floor.

The Italian garden of Warsash House was designed by Sir Frederick Leighton and included a pergola paved in red paviours and covered by virginia creeper, wisteria, clematis and honeysuckle. The casement windows of the conservatory in this view opened into the Italian garden showing the Florentine font.

The pergola walk at Warsash House, with rustic work covered by clematis, wisteria, honeysuckle and virginia creeper. A beautiful sunken rose garden was nearby. At the end of the walk can be seen The Folly, an artistically designed pigeon house.

The Lodge was built of brick with part rough-cast exterior, in pink tint, with tiled roof. It contained a parlour, living room, scullery, larder and three bedrooms, and was connected by telephone to Warsash House.

The clock tower at Warsash, 1916. This clock tower, garage and stable were part of the Warsash House Estate when it was sold in the same year. The clock tower, with its Gillett and Johnson clock, is still one of Warsash's landmarks but the buildings were demolished many years ago and it is now surrounded by a busy thoroughfare.

Stubbington House, 1964. This imposing house was originally constructed in the early eighteenth century, in the reign of Queen Anne, possibly for a member of the Missing family; they are known to have occupied it later in the eighteenth century. In 1841 it became the home of Stubbington House School, started by Revd William Foster. Stubbington House was one of Hampshire's most famous boys' prep schools, with a reputation for being a leading naval school. The school moved to Ascot in the 1960s and the main house was eventually demolished.

Sarisbury Court, 1896. Sarisbury Court was built in 1883 on the site of the former Holly Hill House. In 1896 it was described in the estate agent's particulars as 'an extremely fine modern example of XVI century Renaissance Architecture, built in 1883, and recently reconstructed in the most solid fireproof manner of brick and stone'. It was bought at this time by Sir Edward Walter, the last of the Walter family who had controlled *The Times* newspaper since 1795. It was briefly owned by Sir William Garton of HP Sauce fame, but was eventually demolished in the 1920s.

The hall at Sarisbury Court, 1896.

Seafield Park House, Hillhead. This house was originally built for Sir Frederick Sykes in the early 1870s on land bought from Henry Peter Delme of Cams Hall. It became a private school and then a technical college, which described itself as 'a college for the education of sons of gentlemen for the profession of engineer'. One famous ex-pupil was Thomas Sopwith, the First World War aircraft designer. The building was destroyed by fire in 1947.

Study bedroom at Seafield Park.

Drawing office at Seafield Park.

Price's School hall, 1937. Price's School was
originally established as a charity school in
Fareham by William Price, a local merchant, in
1725. The charity school closed in 1901 but a
new Price's School was built in Park Lane in
1907. It was demolished in 1989.

Price's School physics laboratories, 1937. These laboratories are completely different from those in a modern school! However, Price's School had a very high academic reputation.

BRITAIN IN OLD PHOTOGRAPHS

Margate II
Marlborough II
Marylebone & Paddington
The Melton Mowbray Album
The History of the Melton
   Mowbray Pork Pie
Merton, Morden & Mitcham
Middlesbrough
Around Mildenhall
Milton Keynes
Minehead

The Nadder Valley
Newark
The Norfolk Broads
Norfolk at Work
North Walsham & District
Northallerton
Around Norwich
Nottingham Yesterday
  & Today

Oldham
Ormskirk & District
Otley & District
Oxford Yesterday & Today
Oxfordshire at Play
Oxfordshire at School
Oxfordshire Yesterday & Today

Penwith
Penzance & Newlyn
Around Pershore
Peterborough
Around Plymouth
Poole
Portslade

Prestwich
Putney & Roehampton

Redditch & the Needle
  District
Richmond
Rickmansworth
The River Soar
Around Rotherham
Royal Norfolk Regiment
Rugby & District II
Ruislip
Around Rutland
Around Ryde

Saffron Walden
St Albans
St Andrews
Salford
Salisbury II
Sandhurst & Crowthorne
Sandown & Shanklin
Around Seaton & Sidmouth
Sedgley & District
Sedgley & District II
Sheffield
Sherwood Forest
Shoreham-by-Sea
Lost Shrewsbury
Southampton
Southend-on-Sea
Southwark, Bermondsey &
  Rotherhithe
Southwark, Bermondsey &
  Rotherhithe II
Southwell
Stafford

Around Staveley
Stepney, Bethnal Green &
  Poplar
The History of Stilton
  Cheese
Stockport
Stoke Newington, Stamford
  Hill & Upper Clapton
Stourbridge, Wollaston &
  Amblecote
Stowmarket
Stratford, West Ham & the
  Royal Docks
Streatham II
Stretford
Stroud & the Five Valleys
Stroud & the Five Valleys II
Suffolk
Suffolk at Work II
Sunderland
Sutton
A Swindon Album
Swindon III

Around Tamworth
Along the Thames
Around Thirsk
Tipton
Tipton II
Around Tonbridge
Torquay
Around Truro
Twickenham, Hampton &
  Teddington

Uley, Dursley & Cam
Upminster & Hornchurch

The Upper Fal
Uxbridge 1950–1970

Ventnor

Wallingford
Walsall Revisited
Waltham Abbey
Walton-on-Thames &
  Weybridge
Wandsworth at War
Around Warwick
Weardale
Weardale II
Wednesbury
Wembley & Kingsbury
West Wight
Weymouth & Portland
Around Wheatley
Around Whetstone,
  Totteridge & Finchley
Whitchurch to Market
  Drayton
Wigton & the Solway
  Plain
Willesden
Wimbledon
Around Windsor
Wisbech
Witham & District
The Witney District
Wokingham
The Women's Land Army
Woolwich
Worcestershire at Work
Wordsworth's Lakeland
Wotton-under-Edge to
  Chipping Sodbury

SUTTON'S PHOTOGRAPHIC HISTORY OF TRANSPORT

Jaguar
Jensen & Jensen-Healey
Lotus
Morgan
Rolls-Royce

TVR
Vauxhall
Suffolk Transport
Manchester Road & Rail
Manchester Ship Canal

Black Country Railways
Cheshire Railways
Derbyshire Railways
Devon Railways
Lancashire Railways

Shropshire Railways
Warwickshire Railways
Worcestershire Railways
Steam around Reading
Steam around Salisbury

To order any of these titles please telephone our distributor, Littlehampton Book Services on 01903 828800
For a catalogue of these and our other titles please ring Emma Leitch on 01453 731114